T0196166

Looking For Mr. *Wrong*

Looking For Mr. *Wrong*
(street version)

DAKAR JUSTICE

iUniverse, Inc.
Bloomington

Looking For Mr. Wrong

iUniverse books may be ordered through booksellers or by contacting:

iUniverse
1663 Liberty Drive
Bloomington, IN 47403
www.iuniverse.com
1-800-Authors (1-800-288-4677)

ISBN: 978-1-4759-5733-4 (sc)
ISBN: 978-1-4759-5734-1 (ebk)

Printed in the United States of America

iUniverse rev. date: 11/28/2012

Too many times I hear the same old thing when listening to my women friends-there's a shortage of good black men. But what really is a good black man? I mean they're plenty of black men holding down jobs and taking care of their and sometimes other men's children. But does that mean he's "Mr. Right"? Does the amount of money a man makes, make him a good catch? If a man can dress or looks nice in a suit, does this qualify as a good man? I've asked women what qualities they desire in their ideal man and I basically hear the same things; nice looking, well dressed, respectful, makes good money and isn't a push over-are the main ones. But when I ask them to describe the man they have in their lives now or the guy your dating, I hear just the opposite. Now we've all heard the saying, nice guys finish last and I'm beginning to believe this statement. I know way to many young/older black women "stuck" in their relationship with "Mr. Wrong". And they all say the same thing-'he didn't used to be like this'. So somewhere along the way "Mr. Right" turned into "Mr. Wrong"-but why?

I went and asked a few of my male friends and some guys I really didn't know just to get different opinions on our relationships-most of them surprisingly say they are faithful and like taking care of 'their' girl. So if this is true, lets just say-75% of us are faithful-then what really happens once we both decide to be exclusive? I've been exclusive in all my relationships-(5 to be exact) and I can't say that I've been cheated on in any of them. Now, I have accused my girl once of steppin' out on me but it wasn't confirmed, so I let it go. But who's to say-they all could have. Me personally, I just try my best to have fun and enjoy this person for who they are until they make it impossible for me to do that. I mean, never am I saying I'm perfect or have I always thought this way, but, I've always tried to be as upfront as possible. And until recently, I've just learned to sit back and watch-and if you choose to do some bullshit, then that's on you. I can't allow you to determine how I'm gonna feel on every aspect of life. I was telling a friend of mine a night ago that once a guy decides to give his heart to you, and yall-(ladies)-do something we cant get over, yea we go crazy because we kind of didn't want to do it in the first place. I know that sounds harsh, but ladies always say that they don't wanna get their feelings hurt-so who does?

I believe in love and believe there's certain things you do and certain things you don't do when you're so called-'in love'. And I guess it depends on how you were raised and what you saw growing up which determines how you love and expect love to be given to you. Now, I've had a girlfriend that wanted me to whoop her ass 'cause she was used to that type of shit. I didn't understand at first what was going on, but when I did, I definitely wasn't about start that shit up. I ain't ever hit any women before but I jacked her up against the wall 'cause she's coming at me like a man would. Now in no way do I condone or tolerate any type of abuse to women of any age, color, size, life style or any other bullshit you can throw in there. Believe it or not, I knew niggas beating they girl and when I stepped in the way and said something-she pushed me back. So-I guess she gits what she deserves then-(hope he don't kill'er ass.) I heard many different opinions on this situation from women saying-"you shouldn't step in someone else's relationship no matter how awful it may seem", to guys saying-"every bitch need a good smack every now and then". And I guess that's why domestic abuse is at a all time high and don't seem like its going no where no time soon. I guess some people believe you have to fight for your life or let someone kill you. I don't know if I could know my sister was getting her ass beat on any type of basis and just stand by hoping she fights this nigga back. Because if he did happen to kill her, and I knew this was going on, I would feel responsible for her life ending. But people have the right to believe whatever sick shit they can think of-I guess. So the game is twisted and I'ma keep it as raw as possible 'cause you git tired of hearing 'bout some bullshit and you can't do nothing about it. A few female friends of mine would tell me they getting they ass beat but ain't want me do nothing and I don't understand that shit either. So after while, you don't wanna hear that shit all together. Especially if she really don't want you to do nothing about it. I never understood that type of shit but I guess we're not meant to understand everything we encounter. Now, I don't believe their relationship started off this damn violent so somehow 'Mr. Right' turned into 'Mr. Wrong'. Looking in from the outside, does that mean I can scare her ass into loving me-and only me? I done heard a lot'a old stories 'bout niggas beating or cheating on their wives and the woman choose to stay with'm-so that's nothing new. Somehow it just seams right when your women's doing good for herself and glad to be with you and not 'cause she's scarred of what I might do to her. I did feel at one point I owned my girl, but I got way too many other things going on to be trying to keep up with her all day. I mean a text is good every now and then but lets not git stupid with it. I think its cool to do romantic and spontaneous things and sometimes surprise my girl with different little things. But if I feel she never deserves it, then why be with'er at all-same for the ladies.

I think that most girls do want some type of excitement-(bullshit) in her life, 'cause if ya man doing everything you 'need' him to do, its still gone be a problem. If he's always been respectful and thoughtful of you and kind to everyone you know, then the average chic gone want something a lil' more-(don't lie ladies-yall say that shit now) . . . . Now you might not leave buddy, but you gone cheat on'm, or try to piss him off at some point, so much until he leave or damn near kill yo ass. And that's when you realize how much you really love anigga? I mean maybe I'm meeting the wrong girls but I went to school with a few of'm and they're like sisters, so that shit hurt seeing ya girl beat down like that-(or any young lady) Now, I want to be all my girl wants/ needs at all times-and that's some hard shit to do. So when you think you doing that and she plays you, it's hard to just walk that off. I've heard people say if my girl cheat on me, I wouldn't want to know or I'd stay with'er and just get her back on the low. Well, I guess that's cool if yall been together over 10 yrs or you ain't that cute-but I don't like to be the one hiding and making up lies in shit. I guess I take the fun out'a playing them type of games. Most of the dudes I know, might not cheat on you, but if he do-eventually he gone leave yo ass for hers-(thank about that one). You can call that feeling your way out of

5

the situation. But if she crazier than yo ass, we fall back up out'a that and chill for a while-well that's what I heard . . .

Now it seems like these women I know done got to the point where some nigga hurt'm so much, they now expect it or almost desire it. My old girl wanted to fight so damn much I got tired of going to sleep beside her ass 'cause I'm thanking she gone try to kill me in my sleep in shit. And anther one wouldn't let me get no damn sleep at all, so I didn't give a fuck what nobody talking 'bout at 4:30 in the morning and shit. So now I'm at work tired/pissed off and I know when I git home I ain't gone be able to git no damn rest. So I was the point where I got good at arguing, and we used echo over the whole damn complex-literally. You either know that couple or you are this couple. I'm telling you, I did that shit with babygirl for 2/3 yrs before I just gave it up. She wasn't gonna change. No matter how hard I put in work, she'll do the same shit next couple of days, so that definitely wasn't the problem. Some people are just addicted to arguing and thinking they right all the damn time. That's only cool if you got someone either willing to play that game with you or love the sound of your voice-even if it is saying some dumb shit. Those are two qualities I ain't really picked up yet. (I'm still working on it)

So what's the problem ladies? Why can't you have a good man in your life and believe it? Is it really that bad out here, or is your self confidence low, do to what happened in the past? Or are yall just tired in general and don't even care anymore what the hell we do-you just gone make sure you're good? I mean, I hear that shit a lot now, and I even gotta few old friends trying out this woman on woman thang-(I thank this is the same shit as fucking with niggas-especially if she look like one). But I don't care what nobody do sexually 'cause its your body-just be safe with it. To me, it does seem like a big game we playing and shit, and we all chasing each other for the wrong and obvious reasons-so why add a title then? Especially if you ain't doing nothing but fucking every once in a while anyway. Why do we wanna be with each other, just because the sex so good? And if we do make a relationship out of just sex, does this mean we're using either other for lust? I know some people who think this way as far as-you can't just be fucking somebody and not be with'm-even if you barely know this person. I believe if we really did take the time to git to know each other, we probably wouldn't fucked most of the people we did . . . speaking generally, of course.

But whatever happened to the fall in love and stay that damn way couple? I see a lot of, 'we're doing it just for the look of it-because I put so much work into this shit' couples. Or the, 'no matter what you do-I won't let you leave me' couple. Most of my girls be complaining about how they nigga out doing this and that but they love him even though they doing they thang on the side to. Almost seems like when you git into the relationship you should just go head and get a sneak fuck in-so you don't git totally played. I'm like damn, can anybody be trusted? And most of us all feel the same way 'cause we all say that same shit when we meet, 'nah-that aint me, I wouldn't do that shit'-but what happens some months later?-Its yo ass out there showin' out like kid wit no good damn since. And I'm talking bout grown ass people too, well into they 30's/40's. So is this my future as well, is this what I got to look forward to, still playing them hide in seek games? But now its lie and cheat. And sometimes, people git more than their feelings hurt in the end.

I'm putting this out here cause I know too many beautiful black women in the position of only being happy by themselves and good niggas going to waste-as it seems. I would love to have more children but only with someone I'll hopefully be with forever. And to be honest, I don't believe in love at first sight, so I know it'll probably take some time for me to know she's the right one. I do have a son and as a single man with a kid I don't find if too hard to get dates because I tell you this when I first meet you. Most of the time, a woman will respect a man that will let you know this and that is apart of his child's life. Especially if she has a baby daddy and not a father to her child. Not only do I have a wonderful son, but I am divorced-something I never believed would happen to me. I didn't think I would ever get married and definitely be divorced so this will come up in conversations as well. I haven't really had any problems with that either but I usually don't come across women that I would want to marry or would want to marry me. I usually give off the playa vibe or the non-commitment brotha when I could be both. And yes, I have been both but now I'm kinda just spectating. Call it sideline play calling-although I'd love to get married again, but at this point I'm not looking. (they say that's how you find what you looking for)

I see a lot of us are just passing time or trapped with someone we're in love with but don't really like no more. Most of my niggas really love they girl and she do git on his nerves and I know they do, 'cause we all do stupid shit. But after countless times of trying to git somebody to appreciate you, it do git a lil bit old. Then all of a sudden, somebody start talking to you like you wanna be talked to and treating you like think you should be, and making you feel like you aint felt in a while. So what do you do now-most females I know right now, gone choose to see if that grass is greener. I know yall thank we would to, and you might be right-if you aint doing ya man right. And if you aint-don't trip when he ain't picking up ya calls or returning them text and emails. And if you don't wanna brotha no more, just tell us-but don't try to make us feel like some dumbass-lets be grown ups about it. I've even seen where yall will break up with us and let him still stay there while you out dating and shit. I ain't had that happen, and I don't know how that would work on the other hand, 'cause I'm definitely brangin' somebody home too.

Now I know yall didn't ask for that nigga that broke your heart and made you hate us all, but most of the time yall see the signs and try to 'change anigga' like that's gonna work. That usually only works for the woman after you, she'll reap the benefits of what you had to go through to git this nigga to understand you. Sometimes we just need some space from each other, but most of the time, we just need to leave each other alone. I don't know no nigga that likes a whiney girl and that goes the same for men, women don't wanna hear that sob story shit all the time neither. I think when yall out in the clubs and bars and niggas are approaching you, for the most part, its just a game. You-first of all-wanna be seen gittin' attention and secondly, you wanna see how we gone try you. Most guys no matter how smooth, gone fuck up at some point. And when he do, that's when you make that decision to keep going cause you thank you can put up with this shit-whatever it is. Most of the time this means to us, well I know what I can git away with now, or its no big deal. But eventually that same thing either drives you crazy or some other shit comes up and you can't deal with it, and now you pissed 'cause you been putting up with other shit to begin with. So now, the next time you meet anigga, you gone be almost too picky and wont give him a chance. Or, you so ready to fuck wit the next nigga that say the right thang, you gone head and fall in love with "Mr. Wrong"-again. See the cycle?

I hear a lot of women say you can find a good man in the church but that's a damn lie too. Just 'cause he git up early on Sundays, don't mean he ain't laying it down every other day of the week. Not saying it ain't good brothers in the Lord's house, but don't just believe that's the 'only' place to meet your future husband. And just because anigga on the block, don't mean he doesn't see you as the queen you are. Its just a matter of knowing who you are and what you're willing to put with. To me, you shouldn't have to put up with anything-it should just flow. If it doesn't, then it doesn't, you cant force or make someone fit into your life-even if they look like the perfect match. Sometimes it's the person you thought you wouldn't give the time of day that will be the one that takes you more seriously than you can imagine. And ladies it ain't nothing wrong with gitting ya face out there and meeting a lot of different men, you just ain't gotta fuck all of'm neither-unless you just want to. But what I'm saying is, if you're being real with anigga, no matter what level he on, usually he'll do the same. 'Cause at some point, we all want to know someone's out here who got our back. You just gotta look at the way yall met and sometimes it may be the vibes your putting out that make us try you for the wrong reasons anyway. Now, I don't know that special place to meet "Mr. Right", or I'd tell ya, but if a man approaches you and he confident but a lil unsure of himself too, go ahead and give him a chance-cause we taking chances out here-just by speaking. We know niggas try you everyday on all types of levels and say all types of shit that don't make no sense but we still try. Even if I'm confident you gone give me the number, I'm still a lil nervous 'cause I'm putting myself out here on the judging table and sometimes that's hard to do. And ladies, just because you approach a man don't make you a hoe or nothing-we like to know how yall feeling us. I know ya mama'n'em told ya don't be up in a man face 'cause that gone make him thank he can do whatever he wont to wit you. That's not always a fact-when it comes to people, nothing is always one or the other. There's a lot'a niggas out here ready to give you a commitment and stand up for ya, but yall make it sometimes too difficult just have a simple conversation with you. Now you may be having a bad day, not in the mood or just got out of a bad relationship. Sometimes we sense this and want to correct this, and when we do decide to git at you-we git no love. And just because anigga don't make that much money, don't mean he can't take care of you in other ways. A man is a man, and woman is a woman. What this means is-way before money, God created us-and we all "supposed" love each other regardless of anything else. Maybe this is just my opinion. But I see it all the time, people gitting together for economical reasons. Yea, its hard out here, but what happens if you with somebody you don't really care for, but they take care of you-then you fall in love with somebody else? Shit's wild-I know, happens just about everyday-everywhere. We all making irrational decisions when it comes to being with someone. Sometimes we have to scale that shit out to. Do I want to be loved or taken care of? Now I can't lie, and I've layed up wit a women and she did everything for me-and I really didn't brang nothing to the table. But that never made me feel like a man, so I got my ass up and changed. 'Cause usually or eventually she gone try to control ya ass. If you ain't doin' shit, then she can talk shit-just like niggas do-when we take care of yall. All my niggas did that before-just had some chic lay up and ain't producing shit but some ass-so after while-you do git tired of that shit. It keeps going around and around again.

Donny say we all fall down-I have, so I can understand just about any situation, 'cause I've seen and been apart of some wild shit. I cant say I'm proud of what I've seen/heard/did-but it made me who/what I am today. Some mistakes we make when we choose to deal with certain folks, so its our fault in the end. 'Cause we all know the story on both sides of the fence or been apart of that shit. (I done thrown myself at a chic before and felt dumb-so I learned. I've got numbers I didn't thank I was gone git, called her ass the next day and-wrong number.)

Love is something I thank we all want, no matter how fucked up our

up brangin' was. We were made to love so if our perception is off-so is

the way we're gonna love back. Like I said, we show signs for the most

part we crazy or weird or a lil different. That's why I guess that most

of us keep it simple and go superficial. But most of the time you know

what anigga bout when you meet'm. You know if a man tells you what

you wanna hear 'cause he thinks he got you figured out, that you mite

never git the real man you're looking for in him-'cause he's playing a

roll. So try that nigga that's gone give it to you straight with no extras.

I know a lot of us is putting it down in the bedroom and that's

why its hard to leave anigga. But if that's the only room you gitting

love in, then you need to realize this and decide if this just needs to

be a fuck partner thang. Sometimes falling back can be the best thing

for two people to do. Sometimes, we as men, fall into a relationship

not knowing how much work and time it takes and don't realize this

til we've said the 'L' word or told you-you have our heart. And by this

time-you're wondering why haven't this nigga returned ya text from

a hour ago. Love is a complicated and a very delicate thing that can

brake at almost any given time. The wrong words or actions at the

wrong time can make you wish you never met this person. Now your

wondering how you even loved this fool. Maybe we're all just acting until that moment we realized you do love our stankin' ass-now we don't care about frontin' no more. Don't you hate when you feel like you're the only one in the relationship and nothing you do is noticed? Well, if ya man makes you feel this way, and has been for a while, there's no point in loving by yourself unless you are by yourself. They say its someone out here for everyone, and I do kind of believe this since I've seen people that truly look like they belong together. When I see this, it makes me happy in knowing we are put here to love and grow old with each other. I know a few couples still like that now and it's a beautiful thing to see. Its reported that the black woman is the least likely to get married and that's definitely some terrible shit to hear, especially when they're so many respectable and gorgeous women out here. I know we've all heard the black woman is a lil' attitude-ish but that's not the case all the time. Yes our women go through some 'thangs' and might express them in an aggressive way—but sometimes as black men we can get a lil' wild too. In the end, no matter how forceful she may seem, she just wants to be loved, respected, celebrated and understood.

Now I've been with a few women that had a dominating personality, you just have to assert yourself and let her know you're still the man in this thang. A real woman don't want no push over. Some of my best friends are "bitches" and they know it 'cause we joke about it. But they feel like they can't have some nigga just come in and run their lives and

15

do whatever we want to-cause we will. Now there are women who want to be ran like race horses and I'm sure they'll find a man that will-but to me, that's not sexy. Most niggas do like a lil' shit talk in their girl cause we like a sexy/sassy lady. But when it seems like we just arguing all the damn time, it gits old pretty quick. Now some niggas might like fussin' and fightin' all the time-just make sure he ain't crazy. I know once yall commit to us and put time/work in, you don't wanna hear anything about us looking at other women, but you gotta know this will happen. I mean, we're all visual people and we thrive off of looks, smells and perceptions so when you've upgraded anigga-so to speak-know, women will notice. Whether ya man goes and takes his chances outside of you is his choice, but, make it a hard one for him. Don't buy him a whole bunch of shit and you looking like a bag lady. Keep ya shit together too and compliment ya man, niggas do like that shit. We do think about that kind of stuff when we out there. We ain't all dogs that cant help ourselves when we git around some new pussy-a lot of us just wanna be recognized by our lady. Now you definitely have to make sure your man is physically satisfied-everywhere. And if you do this and still git bad results, then what else can you do-this nigga only in love wit his self. Maybe the only way this will end, is if you finally leave'm. You never know, you might have this brother chasing and wanting you back so bad, he can actually think outside of his self and now can love you.

Sometimes we git so much attention from so many different women its hard to be humble. No need to cuss this man out, just be so cool, that he almost don't believe its you-this will make him think. If all you do is yell at him and take him back, he's going to expect this every time-just like a child with a parent that lets them do anything. You only can git away with what people let you git away with-real shit.

Ladies please don't mama ya man neither. Yea we all need help sometimes but don't make him ya son in shit. Because anigga will git lazy if he know you gone clean up the mess anyway. I believe that's why my marriage didn't work out, she wanted to take control of the whole relationship and I'm like some type of background piece. That's not happening with most men. Now I know how to give my lady the floor when its her turn to have it, but no need to stand behind one another when we can stand right beside each other. Sometimes yall make us feel like its nothing we can do, or everything we're doing is wrong, so at that time-we stop trying all together. And that's were it begins. I don't think you need counseling if yall communicate openly and often. Most of the time we fall out of love because we forget who we fell in love with in the first place, and now you laying across from-this person. Have you ever asked yourself how did I git here with this motherfucker? Yea, its gets crazy sometimes-I know. Some days I go back over all my past girlfriends and try to figure out what I'm doing out here and what do I need to be doing. Now I've done and said some thangs I'm not proud of, but I did'm and gotten over them. The mistakes I made, I wouldn't want anyone else to make them but sometimes that's the only way we know who we are and what we really want. So hopefully wherever you are in life and love, I hope that you're looking forward to only positive outcomes when dealing with counterparts. I know from now on I'm looking for all the signs before I commit so I won't trick myself. I know I've put up with some nonsense just because of some ass or she was so damn this or that. But that don't go so far now, and I don't like to argue back and forth. If we don't agree, then we don't agree. Nothing else needs to be said. I'm not trying to make you somebody else, I want you to be you. And if the you-that you are, isn't what I need, then its no reason to keep holding on to you.

I think a lot of the times, ladies get caught up the swag of a man instead of looking him as a whole person. Just cause he looks nice and may make beautiful kids shouldn't be enough to make him your soul mate. It's a lot of brothers out here with no swag that just need some help in that division that may make the ideal man for you, but you're scared to look outside of ya comfort zone. We have our comfort zones too. We all may need to step outside and take an extra look at what we've been doing and what we should be doing. (If you're wanting a real relationship) I know at one time all my dates were the same girl-just a different color hair. So I switched my circle and went outside of my zone and met all kinds of women I wouldn't have before. Now first impressions may be important, but we're not always ready to meet that possible dream love you've been talking about forever. So give anigga the benefit of the doubt sometimes, cause I don't leave my house thinking I'm gonna meet my Misses Right-ever. Even if I go out to a bar or party or whatever, I'm just going to have a good time and hopefully meet someone that wants to kick it with me. If something comes out of it, then great, but if not, that's fine too.

Now I wasn't blessed with money out the ass and thank God for that because I probably wouldn't been able to handle all the attention I would've gotten. I know for the niggas that are ballin', its hard to be faithful or even trust someone when you're getting so much attention. Not saying all nigas that have cash on delivery have this dilemma, but you can see how this could affect the ego. When you have someone that's taking care of you, so to speak, they might act like they own you or after while, treat you like a dependant. And in relationships, a dependant isn't a good way to look at your other half. Now unless you have the understanding that he's taking care of you because he wants to-then that's different. I have heard of relationships out of convenience and in some cases, this may work out-but of course, this will need to communicated and both of you must know your positions. For the most part, we may know our positions in the relationship but still go out of our way to play private investigator or just leave somebody hanging while they're in love with you. I've heard just about all of my female friends say they go through their man's phone-even when they don't' live together. I think that's insane. If you don't trust this man, or can't trust anyone enough to allow them privacy, then you might have a problem. Whether he messin' with other women or not is his business and how you find out is yours. But I do know that if you start doing shit like this, its hard to stop even when you're on to the next relationship. I think once you git hurt to the point where you want to believe he loves you but you just have to be sure, you're always looking to be disappointed somehow. And if you don't find anything suspicious, will this stop your curiosity towards him, and could you just allow him to love you? With all this technology we have like cell phones, emails, face book-twitter and all the other sites we have, it is becoming easier to be some type of space age pimp. And yes niggas is taking advantage of these things as well as the ladies. Me personally, I don't have the time or the will to check behind my girl. And I don't want a girl who's always trying catch me in a lie. If we've been together for a while and you still feel like I'm giving you a reason not to trust me, I'll make it easy and leave you alone. Why keep trying to convince someone you love them all the time and no matter what you do-it's never enough?

I remember times as to where I felt like I wanted to cheat on my girl and actually having the chance to-but didn't because I wasn't ready to leave her. I always believed that once you start looking outside the relationship then its kind of over at that time so I tried to just keep it fresh with my girl at all times. I did get to the point where I went over this girls house with the intensions of cheating on my lady. My co-worker was sitting on my lap and kissing me when something in my head said, 'this ain't right' and I needed to thank about this before I go all the way. And on the way over to her crib I tried not to thank about what I was about to do and just keep it cool. Everything was cool 'til I realized that I was going to have to go back home to my girl with this other girl's scent all on me. Now yea, I could've took a shower but that still wouldn't washed off what we did. I didn't tell her how close I had got to anther girl but it did make me appreciate her more and want to be a better man. She was getting on my nerves at the time but she was also helping me out with my job and letting my driver her car. So yea I did owe it to her not to play her out like we do so many times. I heard some fowl stories of what my girls allow us to do to them and sometimes its so crazy-it is funny. But its never really funny when dealing with someone's emotions and feelings toward you. Its hard to believe sometimes love makes you do dumb-ass shit. I know all to well, I've done some things I never would've imagined to let some girl know I was hers-and needless to say, I'm not with any of these ladies now.—So was it worth it? Well, for me it was 'cause I now know how far I'm willing to embarrass myself and how far I will go to show my love for you. Not saying I won't go all out for you, but why should I have to keep trying to prove to you how much I love you when I know and everybody else knows-but you?

I believe as black men, we need to feel we are important and in a meaningful relationship with our women. We need purpose. I think that once a man decides to just allow his woman to take over or control the relationship, we loose ourselves in some way. We, as men, are used to being the provider or the bread winner so if that's taken away from us, then what's our purpose with this woman. If we feel you don't need us, then any nigga can just come up in here and make this his home-for the most part-when this may not be the case at all. In the '90's, there was a corporate movement for the black woman, so to speak, as to where she was getting the job or position that could basically take care of the entire household. In a way, this was monumental to the community but almost destructive to the home. Now, in a time where we should be celebrating our women's growth in being noticed as vital part of society-we now are envious or resentful of the same woman that's been supportive of us since time began. Its almost like-what am I good for if I can't even take care of my woman. There are some guys who totally don't mind their lady being the primary source of income, and aren't leaching off of them either. But for most of us, we have to have the title of bread winner or we feel impotent somehow. I've asked some ladies how they feel about making more than their man and mostly I hear it doesn't matter, unless she's making over a certain amount and this amount varies for all women. Most women just want to know that by any chance something happens to them or their career-we can step in and handle everything on our own. Understandable, but for most average guys, there's no certainty in what we're doing and that's frustrating enough by itself. So now there's a divide or gap between us financially and she's out in the world helping shape it, and we're just in it. I hear a few men say, they don't mind their wife cakin' it up. But the male ego is very fragile and sometimes we think we can handle our lady taking care of us-when we really can't. So for the woman who has it all and a man who's still trying to find his way-what does she do?—Remain as supportive as she can and keep pushing him in the right direction. Because we all hate to be reminded of the situation we're stuck in. I even felt at one point like I wasn't bringing nothing to the table when my girl sat me down and made me see how important the little things I was doing helped her out. Like-just because I couldn't brang the groceries home, I cooked for her and also washed up after we ate. I might not of been able to take her where she wanted to go on her birthday, but I bathed her, gave her a massage, I wrote her a poem and made her feel like the queen she is. And that didn't cost anything. I know all guys ainn't gonna do the same exact things I did, but just being thoughtful and basically just being there should be enough to make ya woman proud to have you. The little things do mean a lot more than we understand, and as men, we need to be reminded of this sometimes.

For the woman that has a man in her life that just doesn't get it or he doesn't want to-its up to you to either make this nigga take you more seriously or up and leave. To be honest, a relationship is a job and if you really don't like this job, then you need to find anther one-why settle? A dead end relationship isn't helping nobody in the end, especially the kids. We all 'want' the person that helped make this child in their lives or living wit them-but if this isn't on his agenda, don't try to force it on him. He'll either grow up and realize what life is or maybe not-this isn't your fault. Hopefully, he'll grow to see what he's missing out on. God works, whether we believe or not. Whether this man is willing to own up to his mistakes or willing to take responsibility for his actions, is on him and him only. Most of us who don't take care of our own, it comes back on us in various ways and we wish we could go back in time and change things. Sadly, its usually too late or we never git the chance to be that father we should've been-and that hurts more than a slap in the face. I was raised by my mother for several years by herself before she got married-and she wasn't perfect-but she was there. You can say we learned together-how to grow, because she didn't know what to do when raising a man-but somehow she did. One thing I can say about my mama is that, she never had a lot of niggas in and out of the crib and she didn't tolerate no bullshit from nobody. This made me feel like it was just us at times-and it was. She moved 1700 miles away from my father because she thought this was the best thing for us. And it may have been. Not saying I didn't need to know this man, but maybe the shit he was doing-she knew I shouldn't have seen or heard about. I can now understand and respect the decision she made and though she was 17 at the time-it was the second biggest one she ever made. The first was having me wit this man. She told me later what type of man he was and why she choose to leave him. I know she was only concerned with my future as a productive/positive black man-and at the time, my father was neither and not on the path of becoming this either. 'Til this day, I've haven't met him, but we've spoke on the phone once/twice. I don't feel like I've missed out on too many things because I had to learn them on my own, which helped me-I believe become this strong today. I don't want any of you to believe not having ya child's father in the picture is a good thing, unless this man is harmful to you or the child. Some people aren't meant to be great parents though they've made wonderful kids. It may be your right to see your children, buts it's still a privilege that can be taken from you if you don't deserve it. Any man who has to be forced or constantly reminded to see or do for his child/children doesn't really want this in his life anyway, so why frustrate yourself and confuse the kids. And allowing your kids to see mommy and daddy fighting all the time definitely isn't helping the situation-its hurting your kids. And we all know how the cycle of life works, we usually emulate what we grow up around. Our surroundings are all we know until we're able to go outside of our environment. Rarely, we stray away from what our parents do in the household and make good/rational decisions despite having immature parents. So don't bank on them growing up being better than you if you're making poor decisions-it might not work out like this.

I feel we all need to be more honest with ourselves when trying to deal wit each other. To me, a relationship shouldn't be a-what can you do for me-type thing unless that's the only relationship you're both seeking. If you want a serious commitment with a man you should express this with this man and listen to exactly what he communicates to you. Most of the time yall think you've found the one and he's telling you he's not, or doesn't want to be, but you already have this future planned out for us. For the most part, we don't like to have our whole lives put into a daily planner or mapped out for us. We like being in the driver seat but want to know that our passenger's willing to go where ever we go, even if we're just cruising aimlessly. We know you live off of certainties, and we do also, but just on a different scale. Sometimes we don't care where we end up, just as long as you're there with us-it doesn't matter where we go. To most women, that's sounds good but still isn't enough to keep you secure in knowing what tomorrow's gonna be. Even if you have a time frame or certain things you want to see happen-don't force is on us, because we don't wanna feel rushed or like we're on your time. I know every woman has this fairy tale dream of her ideal man and the way your lives play out, but most of us can't fit into this mold. Most of the time, that shits unrealistic anyway or its far fetched and we're just looking to be a 'normal' couple. I can see how you may have been made to feel like this fantasy love is owed to you, but in the real world, many of us are just surviving and want a "stable" relationship when everything else isn't. And when you do find the man of your dreams and he can take you away from this harsh reality, what do you do when the high comes down? Because it will come down. Now you're gonna have to deal with this man and on a real scale. If you're a superficial woman and only want material things, it can be a rude awakening if this man looses everything but you. So are you going love this man now, or help him back on his feet? Well, if you never loved him, you probably won't now, so you'll just keep it moving. But for the sistah that doesn't care what a man owns, this will be the time that you'll show ya strength and love. And that's all a real man wants to know anyway-that his girl is with him for who he is and not what he has. Sometimes a man just needs a good woman to help jumpstart or motivate him and push us in the right direction.

If you feel like you're competing with ya man's mom, you shouldn't. You should never git in the middle of ya man and his mother's relationship even though there are some guys who seem like they can't make a move without her involved. Sometimes this may be the only female's voice he's had in his head and it gits hard to hear you. He may know you love him, but she's been there since birth and her opinion may be the pillow he's used to sleeping on. Don't be scarred or bothered by this, even if she doesn't particularly like you. Mothers generally don't like anyone their son's brang home, and 9 times out of 10-you won't either. Now ya man should have his own back bone and shouldn't need to call her and ask for her approval on everything. But if you feel like he's going down this path, then maybe you should talk-not fight-about how this makes you feel as his partner. Most guys can't communicate with women on a emotional level or can't express certain things because of how other ladies may have judged or treated them in the past. This is where you come in-now you can open doors that no other woman has. You can be that one and only girl outside of mommy that he now has the chance to share intimacies with. This can take yall to new heights. We usually don't open up to fast because we are sensitive creatures, despite how hard he may seem on the outside. We all have the same chemical make up, even if we don't show or use these feelings aloud. Most of the time, it's the ones who act like they never had feelings that are hurting the most and suffering inside. If we break down and tell you our intimacies and you take is as a joke, you might not git the opportunity to view that side of us again. Now you've just lost the real side of this person, and finding him may be impossible now. Some women never git to see that side of their man, and if they do-its almost like meeting this person for the first time-not the one everyone thinks they know. This can make both of you stronger and better lovers all around.

When I tell people I've had three relationships that lasted at least 5 years, they can't believe it. I started finding out about love around 14/15-jumping in head first and crashing hard. Didn't know what I was gitting into-but once I felt that she felt me, I almost couldn't believe that a woman outside of my moms loved me like that. My first 'real' love was one of the most life changing and extraordinary things I've ever dealt with. And 'til this day I think about how she still affects me, how she made me see the things I do about women and she was only 15 then, too. I've always had that me against the world attitude, so when I found a girl who felt the same way and was willing to fight the world for me-as I for her, I took that to the heart. We used talk major shit to each other but I loved it. I only took one thing she said to heart and said something back just to hurt her. That's when our whole thing changed-well at least for me it did. I never meant to hurt this young woman-but I did. I don't remember what she said that made me feel so childish, but I told her she'd never find love. And I still regret ever letting those words come out my mouth or even thinking this shit. She was, and still is a great person and deserves love just like we all do. I was 17 when I said this and from that point, I always think before I say anything-especially when arguing. I try just to say what I mean and not shit just to hurt you. For some reason, when you're just trying to hurt someone's feelings, and you do-you still don't feel good, or I don't at least. So if you got that slick tongue, be careful what you say with it, cause life is a lil less fun when you're alone. This is why I don't like arguing too much. You can express yourself without hurting someone else, even when you're pissed off. But most of the time, we're looking to hurt that person. Just know that once you do, the consequences can leave you regretful.

I know a lot of my sistahs are looking out for their man-watching his back from the law. That's cool and you should cause that's ya man. When I was out there running the streets, my girl would say shit like she's getting tired of not knowing whether I'd make it back home and gitting that call. The one where she'd need to come identify my body, and I didn't totally understand that. When you're out there gitting money and you young, you ain't thinking about the ones that love you unconditionally. You're not thinking you'll ever be the one that doesn't make it back-it just happens. And when it does happen, and you're left to pick up the pieces, and whatever the outcome-its tough. If we hustling 'cause we feel like we have to and it ain't no other way to git money, then we definitely need your support. But if you never like that lifestyle in the first place, yea its gonna affect you in a negative way and make you say shit that he don't wanna hear. Some niggas do got felonies and may have gotten them by being the wrong place/wrong time type thing or may have been wild but learned from our mistakes. But if society doesn't give him the chance to prove himself, then it's hard to just not do nothing. At least ya man is motivated to make his own money. I know a few chics that say they tired of that D-boy shit, and yall have the right to feel however you do. But don't thank he gonna be a working class nigga overnight. It might take years for him to find a honest or steady job. Its hard out here for everyone, even people who don't have records. So if you've argued about this for the kids sake or ya own personal concerns then you have to understand most people do what they know best or what come easily to them. Try to help ya man on this job search instead of just telling him what he need to do. If this don't work or you already tried, try again. Now if you tried and tried and you tired now, make up ya mind on what you gone do and stick to ya guns. Money is money they say-it don't matter where it come from. But if money ain't ya concern, you more worried about you and the child's safety, then please remove yourselves from the situation. If he love his kids or/and you, he'll be there-and if not, just know you did the right thing for yall. Sometimes you gotta see the future so you can make the right decision today in order to have a tomorrow.

I really do love and want my all my sistas to be happy out here cause I see yall working hard and doing ya thang and I no you'd appreciate someone that appreciates you. I know that we sometimes look at you like machines or objects, but we know we need you when it comes down to it. I see so many smart/sexy women holdin' down a job or career with kids and running a household. That's never been no easy thing to do, so salute yourself if you don't have no one to recognize this. I know sometimes you git frustrated and want to quit, especially when you have a man or you're supposed to have one and he's non-existing. It's no fun and harder holding down a household by yourself and you're not alone. I also know way too many of us are in a failing marriages and don't have the courage to correct this shit. We just put up wit so much shit to the point where it almost feels like we deserve it. I wonder if somehow we, deep down, do need this pain to make us feel whatever it is we need to-to feel loved. Maybe love is supposed to hurt sometimes, just like life, so you can appreciate the good times you do share with each other. Maybe we need the bad times to remind us of what we've overcame. But there still has to be some type of cut off or boundary where you know this is just a lil too complicated or just plain bullshit. And having a 'just for the lack of an argument' type of attitude isn't really gittin' nobody nowhere. That means, if he don't wanna talk to you at all, he wins cause he gone get what he want all the time. He's happy or pleased while you stressed out-holding it in. Stress will kill yo ass, no jokes-for real. Nobody wants to be in a void or stale relationship, and nobody wants to be so aggravated by their partner they literally can't stand them. Start breathing different when they come around or ya blood pressure goes up, these thangs can kill you eventually. Or cause you to have all types of physical damage. And the longer you live, the more I'm sure you hear these things happing to us-this isn't coincidental at all. We joke about it all the time saying shit like, 'one day she gone kill yo ass, or he gone be the death of me' and that shit really can be true. You gotta be smart for yourselves and the kids, if any. If you don't have any kids with this dumb-ass nigga, Love, you really wasting ya time. And you cant git time back no matter how much you pray. That's why there's so many bitter-ass old people now-don't be one of them. They done forgot what the hell happiness is and now don't wanna see anybody happy. Sometimes love will kick you up and down the block-and that's because you let it. So stop trippin' off that shit and start over. Maybe, first work on yourself for a while. You must love yourself first and foremost before you could ever love somebody else successfully. 'Cause if you don't know your worth heaven, everyone's gonna be glad to give you hell. That's just the way it works unfortunately and most of us are living testimonies of this-sad to say.

All my ladies in a dead end relationship, you should definitely fall back and take a long look at yourself. Whatever is causing you to believe you deserve this type of treatment, you need to revaluate this in depth. Maybe its due to the lack of love as a child or it may be what you've seen growing up. I know way too many young women allowing us to mentally and physically abuse them. Name calling and shit talking can be cute until it gets out of control to the point where yall actually wanna hurt each other. Just know that if you allow this man to beat you like a dog, then that's exactly what you are to him . . . . a dog. Same thing goes for the opposite-if you have a man that will treat you like a treasure-then that's what you must be. Even if you haven't found the one that's willing to do this, that doesn't mean you're not worth it or we're not out here-we are, and we're looking for you. Make yourself available and make it known what you want and follow up with what you say. Don't just talk the talk. 'Cause that will cause us to play that game if we're up to it-and you'll be in the same place again . . . . stuck wit "Mr. Wrong".

I was talking to a friend of mine who's in a on-again/off again relationship and she says she thinks too many women put up with anything just to keep a man. I agree to a certain degree. I see it all the time and have heard a lot of wild stories which happen to be sadly true. A friend of mine just found out her longtime boyfriend had another baby on the side while living with her. She, at first, threw him out and stuck to her guns by not talking to him, accept for when he gets his kids. After a month or so, she started back the same old same thing again and he's back in the house and doing the same shit to her again. She confided in me and told me how much she loves and understands him. Which is a wonderful thing, but he's not responding to her the way she needs him to. Clearly, if he's out making other children with different women, he's not on the same page or even in the same book as her. I hate to see how this makes her feel as a person, let alone someone's partner. She works hard at her job and does basically what she needs to do to hold the home down, and all she wants is to be reciprocated. I'm sure there's a wide variety of ladies that are in the same boat looking for a soul mate. I'm no expert on love, but I do know how you should and shouldn't be treated in a monogamous liaison. I've been in quite a few commitments and I've heard pretty much the same things when dealing with my sistahs and they just want to be understood and loved unconditionally.

Now I believe we get the term unconditional misconstrued when it comes to bonding with someone outside of our family. Not saying loving someone with no limitations isn't great, but it can be very tiresome. Especially if this person doesn't feel or act the same towards you. We've all done things we're not proud of, but if were willing to share this with you, then that's a start because its hard to put yourself out there. Once I let all of the past mistakes of my partner go, I just tried to only look to the future with her. If you're with someone who can't get past your past or you can't git past theirs, then you may be with the wrong person. We can't go back an undo the wrongs, we only can move forwards-so if this person won't allow you growth, they're holding you back. If you can't let his past go, then let him go-that's the best thing for both of you. No one wants to be reminded of who or what they used to be, if they've changed. Sometimes when we're 'with' someone, we tend to want to keep them in the light we want to see them in and when they grow out of what we're used to, this scares us. Your partnership should grow and blossom into something special and you both should adore and respect this growth. If you're both growing into opposite directions, then this can destroy communication boundaries. Once communication is gone, so is the bond. If you're not bonding, then you're not growing as a team. I like to look at relationship as a team effort and you can't win if you're not playing together as one. As a team, you'd uphold your side of the deal and so should your partner. Yea, we all get tired and beat down by life and that's when your team mate steps up and takes on some of your responsibility. This should be a continuous thing that both of you practice, not just you all the time holding up their end. Don't allow yourself to be played.

Allowing yourself to get played is what most women do when it comes having a man in their lives. What I'm saying is, if a man knows you need a man, he's more likely to 'try' you, to see how far he can go. This is human nature so don't go blaming him right away. Your man can only do what you let him do. I know you've heard this before and this is the truth. Not saying you're his probation officer but you can't be a pushover or never asserting yourself as an "equal" partner. All men want to feel like the man in the relationship but this doesn't mean he's in control of everything yall do-or visa versa. In a mutual agreement, both of your should have some say-so on what makes both of you happy. No one wants to feel like a parent to their lover and if so, this may be a problem. Some people do like to be mothered or fathered, but don't let this get out of hand. If you are a controlling person, don't just accept it-work on it. You may have someone that really wants to do right by you but doesn't want to feel belittled. We all have important qualities that should and need to be recognized.

I also hear my ladies saying since their man doesn't recognize her qualities anymore, they're gonna step out on them or make them jealous. This usually doesn't work out for the good of the relationship. I mean, why play games with someone's emotions when you could be finding the person that's truly meant for you. When you git to the point where you have to do things for your man to notice you, maybe its not you that's the problem. I know most relationships do get stale, so both of you should be trying to figure out what you can do to keep it brand new. If this is something you both are willing to work on and build, then it shouldn't be a problem sitting down and talking about it. A lot of the time, we as men, get very comfortable or content in our ways. This may take affect on you after a while and we might not even notice the signs. Its not that we don't love you, we just see things differently. And yes we should notice that you've changed hairstyles or bought a new dress or what have you, but by going out and having another man on the side aint a solution at all. I know sometimes keeping a partnership fresh is a hard as hell, but its something you'll have to work on. No relationship is perfect but there are perfect people for each other in all different demographics, so why should you be stuck in an ongoing feud?

As I said, I do know people who are in great relationships and when I ask them how they do it, I always hear-trust and communication are key. And I agree with this because without trust how can you believe anything your partner has to say? And if you can't communicate, how do you know who you're with? People change everyday whether they know it or not. Sometimes the things we see or are involved with may cause our thinking to change and today I feel totally different from yesterday. Your partner may not have witness or experienced what you have, and this could cause a wedge between you. If you've been out and doing or seeing new things and your partner hasn't, this can divide you or cause jealously to intervene. Becoming a new person or finding yourself while in a failing relationship shouldn't be something to look down upon. This may be what God intended for you and only you. Your partner may not understand this and may not need to. Two people can start out being the best friends and somehow drift apart and it's on one's fault. When defining yourself, your commitment to this other person should only be part of who you are, not all that you are.

If you don't have a life outside of this person, this can be detrimental of harmful to you as a person. You both should have an outlet outside of this partnership if you want it to be a healthy one. Its noting wrong with wanting to lay up under your man, but there positively needs to be time where you guys miss each other. Missing someone's touch, smell or voice can keep things interesting and you won't get bored often. Try to do things or go out without each other sometimes and give space to your man. Spend the weekend with a girlfriend, sister or your mother and check up on him very little. Make him miss you and I bet he'll be calling and checking up on you more than you thought. We tend to get lost without our girl whether we're man enough to admit it or not. No matter how macho we may act, if we really love you, a weekend will seem like forever and we can't wait for you to get home. I mean seriously give a weekend to himself and the kids and let him worry about you. This may be what yall been missing. And sometimes, you guys just need a break from one anther. A break isn't a bad thing or something to viewed as negative, its just anther way to keep it fresh. Every so often we all get tired of the rigmarole; the tedious events of life and just need a rest. To have time to yourself or time to recuperate, is a very positive thing indeed. Once stress starts to seep into your everyday life, any little thing can cause an explosion that can alter how you see each other. Sometimes we do say things we don't mean, but don't allow yourself to always get pissed before your say something you've been meaning to. Meaning, if you have a problem with something he's said/done, don't wait 'til you're mad, then bring it up. Two people yelling won't help any situation, especially if neither of you are listening to what yall are actually saying. Try waiting 'til he's in a relaxed mood and ease ya way into whatever it is that frustrates you and give clear examples of why this frustrates you. You never know, he might understand you and want to please his girl instead of git on ya nerves.

I do believe that any communication is better than none at all. But I don't condone endless fussing/fighting and threats. Some doors you open can't be closed with just an apology. So when you are in a heated moment, and your feelings might of gotten hurt, you should still try your best to maintain some type of dignity. I know once you've heard something you totally disagree with, its almost impossible to keep listening and allow them to continue, but sometimes that's the only time we can truly say what we've been wanting to. This isn't the way we should go about saying important things and we shouldn't have to yell to get our point across. If this is the only way he can say what he truly means or this sounds like you, maybe you guys need counseling. There's no need to for yall to damn near kill each other in order to be heard. If you can't just sit down and talk about real things as grownups, then maturity will need to be present on someone's part. If neither one of yall are ready to be mature adults, then both of you need to part ways and do some growing up.

When it comes down to it, are you really ready to support and love someone outside of yourself? This is the ultimate question. If you do believe you are and you know you're worth being loved, its time to start looking for something real and permanent. But before you hit the clubs or bars or wherever you choose to go, make sure you are mentally stable enough to handle a serious guy. Meaning, don't bring your last or any past relationship into a new one. Of course your going to remember all the things that got you to this point in you life but don't keep reminding us and yourself of what already happened. If you keep going back, you never move forwards. We all had someone hurt us, but this person can't and will not be in everybody you meet. Remember, there are good men out here who just want the simple things in life as you. We want love, respect and to know that who we're with, is with us too-because they want to be with us. With all the bullshit life can conjure, it's a beautiful thing to know that you have someone that can't wait to see you. One of the best feelings is to know that you have the ability to make someone feel important and in doing this, you're rewarded back in the same way. I do believe God put us all here to love in some sort of fashion and we all have our ways about us which makes it difficult but exiting once you've found this special someone.

So for the single lady out there that has a world of love to offer and no one to share with, don't get frustrated and give up or stop caring.

Closing the door on a lifetime of love can be a very long and lonely life. There's so many interesting single men just waiting to be found and explored and we know the pain of the past and want a chance at reversing this soreness you may be holding onto. So take your time to look at us as an individual and not in general because one mistake isn't all our doing. And if you are still hurting from what someone did, take time to let this heal and be prepared for "Mr. Right" once he does enter your atmosphere. You never know, he may sitting next to you now-just waiting to be to one who shows you how wonderful true love can be. Good luck and much success/happiness to you all!